Chinese Australians

Book 2

Early Chinese Migrants

The First Chinese Australians

Marji Hill

Published by The Prison Tree Press 2025

Copyright © 2025 Marji Hill

The Prison Tree Press
Suite 124
1-10 Albert Avenue
Broadbeach, Queensland 4218
https://marjihill.com

ISBN: 9781763738447   Hardback
ISBN: 9781763738454   eBook

 A catalogue record for this book is available from the National Library of Australia

All rights reserved. No part of this book may be reproduced, stored in a retrieval system, or transmitted in any form or by any means, electronic, mechanical, photocopying, recording, scanning, or otherwise, without the prior written permission of the publisher.

Disclaimer:

All the material contained in this book is provided for educational and informational purposes only. No responsibility can be taken for any results or outcomes resulting from the use of this material.

While every care has been taken to trace and acknowledge copyright the publishers tender their apologies for any accidental infringement where copyright has proved untraceable.

Every attempt has been made to provide information that is both accurate and effective, however, the author does not assume any responsibility for the accuracy or use/misuse of this information.

Acknowledgement is given to Canva for most of the illustrations in this book. The paintings, however, were created by Marji Hill.

THE SERIES

Chinese Australians

Book 1

Australia and China

Before Captain Cook

Book 2

Early Chinese Migrants

The First Chinese Australians

Book 3

Chinese and Gold

the Chinese on the Australian Goldfields

Book 4

The Chinese Experience

The Untold Story of Prejudice and Violence on the Australian Goldfields

Book 5

The Chinese Legacy

How Migration, Culture and Community have Influenced Australia

Acknowledgements

I acknowledge the Traditional Custodians
of Country throughout Australia
and their connections to land, sea, and community.

I pay my respect to elders, past, present, and emerging
and extend my respect to all First Nations peoples today.
In the spirit of reconciliation,
my mission is to increase understanding
between the First Nations and other Australians
and to provide people from all over the globe
some basic understanding of Australia s first people,
their history, and cultures.

In addition,
I thank Eddie Dowd for helping me get this book
into its final form for publication.
I also acknowledge the support
from John and Sherien Foley.

Marji Hill

Table of Contents

1.	A World Far Away	1
2.	The First Chinese in Australia	3
3.	A Man Named Mak Sai Ying	5
4.	Life in China in the 1800s	7
5.	Leaving China	11
6.	Why Did They Come to Australia?	13
7.	The Australian Land Clearing Company	17
8.	What Work Did They Do?	19
9.	Was Life Easy?	21
10.	Resistance and Racism	23
11.	The Growing Chinese Community	25
12.	A Look Ahead	27
13.	Remembering the Past	29
14.	Timeline	31
GLOSSARY		33
SOURCES		35
ABOUT MARJI HILL		37
MORE BOOKS BY MARJI HILL		39

1. A World Far Away

Imagine living in a small village in southern China in the 1800s.

Your family grows rice, fishes in the rivers, and gathers food from the land. Life is hard. There are floods, not enough food, and not enough jobs.

Rice harvesting

Your parents say, "There is a land across the sea called Australia. If you go there, you might find work and earn money to help us."

And so begins the journey of early Chinese migration to Australia.

Chinese people first began coming to Australia in small numbers in the early 1800s. It was not until the 1850s that thousands more arrived, especially during the gold rush.

But long before that, a few brave men made the journey and began new lives in a faraway land.

2. The First Chinese in Australia

In 1788, with the arrival of the First Fleet from England, the course of Australian history was changed forever. The British started building their colony in Australia.

At the time, ships were travelling between Australia and China to trade goods. Sometimes these ships needed new crew members. Chinese sailors were hired at Chinese ports like Canton (now called Guangzhou) and Xiamen (Amoy).

When ships from Australia were in Chinese ports, they often hired Chinese sailors to replace sailors who had died or who had deserted ship.

When some of these sailors arrived in Australia they chose to stay in Sydney. They might have been paid off or left the ship.

A few found work in Sydney and settled there. These early arrivals were the first Chinese Australians.

Records show that around 18 Chinese people had settled in Australia before 1848. While that might not seem like a lot, they were the brave pioneers who helped start the Chinese Australian story.

3. A Man Named Mak Sai Ying

One of the first Chinese settlers we know about was Mak Sai Ying, also called John Shying.

He arrived in Australia in 1818 on a ship named *Laurel*. He was born in Guangdong, a coastal province in southern China. Mak Sai Ying worked as a carpenter—someone who builds with wood. He worked for important people like John Blaxland and Elizabeth Macarthur, whose husband helped start Australia's wool industry.

Mak Sai Ying opened The Golden Lion Hotel, a pub (public house) in Parramatta and owned several businesses. He married an Irish woman named Sarah Jane Thompson and they had four sons. After Sarah passed away, he went back to China but later returned to Australia and married again.

Mak Sai Ying's story shows that Chinese migrants worked hard and became part of Australian life early on.

4. Life in China in the 1800s

China in the 1800s was ruled by an emperor.

It was known as the Chinese Empire which had been a powerful country for hundreds of years.

Chinese Emperor

But things were changing.

China had a very large population. In 2025, the Chinese population was 1.4 billion people – the largest population in the world! But even back in the 1800s, there were already many millions of people living there.

**China in the 1800s had been
a powerful country for centuries**

Most people were peasants and lived in small villages. But many families were struggling. There was poverty and famine. There was not enough work, food, or land. Some people lost their homes because of war, floods or robbers.

Life in China was becoming more difficult. Apart from the floods, famines, and civil wars in the countryside, gangs of armed men attacked villages. Some families lost their homes, crops or even their lives.

The government was weak, and people were unhappy. Many dreamed of leaving and starting a better life somewhere else.

Young men were encouraged to go overseas, work hard and send money home to help their families.

5. Leaving China

Most people had never left their village, let alone travelled across the ocean. The journey to Australia took many weeks or even months. The ships were crowded and uncomfortable.

Leaving China was not easy

Men travelled alone. They were not allowed to bring their wives or children with them.

Some paid for the journey with their own money. Others used credit tickets — this meant they borrowed money for the trip and had to repay it by working in Australia.

Some men even promised their land or asked their families to take responsibility if they could not repay the debt.

Travelling from China to Australia

Even though it was risky and scary, many were willing to take the chance for a better future.

Just a few Chinese people came to Australia between 1800 and 1850.

Early Chinese Migrants

6. Why Did They Come to Australia?

As a new colony, Australia needed workers.

In 1840, Britain stopped sending convicts to Australia. This caused a shortage of labour.

Farmers and business owners needed help to clear land, build roads and grow crops.

Chinese worker

Early Chinese Migrants

Chinese workers were known to be hardworking, so British companies began hiring them. They were brought over as servants, artisans or general labourers and were welcomed in the heavily under-populated Australia.

The first group of cheap indentured labourers arrived in October 1848 from Xiamen (Amoy), in China's southeastern province of Fujian. There were 120 of them, 100 adults and 20 boys, and they were soon followed by others.

They included both indentured or contracted labourers and free emigrants.

Between 1848 and 1853, over 3,000 Chinese workers came to Australia

Indentured labourers meant they had to sign contracts to work for several years.

Between 1848 and 1853, over 3,000 Chinese workers came to Australia. Most worked in the countryside. They cleared land, built irrigation ditches (channels to carry water), and helped farmers grow crops. Some became cooks, gardeners or fishermen.

Together, these two forces — the push from China and the pull from Australia — helped shape early Chinese migration to Australia.

7. The Australian Land Clearing Company

One Chinese company that helped workers come to Australia was the Australian Land Clearing Company. It was based in Tuishan County in southern China.

The company hired workers and paid for their travel. But the men had to pay the company back after they started working. If they did not repay, their families in China were held responsible.

Although this system was tough, it helped many men get to Australia, find work and support their families back home.

The idea of leaving China was not easy. Travel was dangerous and most people had never left their village. Still, thousands of young men decided to take the risk.

Most came alone. The Chinese government and companies such as the Australian Land Clearing Company did not allow them to bring their wives or children.

This regulation was tough and difficult but it also meant that if the men could not repay their travel debts, their families back in China would be responsible.

Some men paid for their journey themselves. Others came on credit tickets, which meant they borrowed money for the trip. They often had to promise their land or even their family as security.

Once in Australia, they had to work hard and send money back to repay the loan.

The journey by sea was long but the promise of a better life kept their hopes alive.

8. What Work Did They Do?

Chinese workers did many different jobs. They cleared bushland to make space for farms. They built roads, wells, and ditches for water. Others worked as shepherds taking care of sheep or planted gardens to grow fruit and vegetables. Some worked as tradesmen like carpenters or cooks. Their knowledge of farming and water helped them turn dry land into green gardens.

Some planted gardens to grow fruit and vegetables

They often moved from one job to another, carrying all their belongings. They travelled in groups, cooked together, and looked after each other.

9. Was Life Easy?

No.

Life in Australia was not easy for Chinese workers.

They worked long hours and were often paid less than others. They lived in small huts or tents near their job sites. Because they could not bring their families, many were lonely. They missed their homes and wrote letters to their loved ones, sending money whenever they could.

But even with these hardships, many Chinese migrants managed to build better lives. Some started their own businesses or market gardens. These gardens sold fresh vegetables to towns and helped feed local people.

10. Resistance and Racism

Although Chinese workers were brought to help build the colony, not everyone welcomed them.

Some British settlers did not like the Chinese because they were different. They looked different, spoke another language, and had different customs.

The Chinese looked different from the Europeans

People began to complain that Chinese workers were taking jobs from others. Newspapers and public meetings said unkind things about them.

This was the beginning of racism toward Chinese people in Australia.

Sadly, racism would become worse in the years ahead — especially during the gold rush in the 1850s.

11. The Growing Chinese Community

As more Chinese workers arrived, small communities began to grow. The men worked, saved money, and helped each other. Some started small businesses and set up shops or food stalls. Others became cooks or traders.

Chinese boarding house

By 1850, entire ships were arriving with Chinese passengers. Around one-third of them paid their own way. The others borrowed money or used credit tickets.

These early Chinese migrants helped build towns and farms. They brought new foods, ideas, and skills to the young Australian colonies.

12. A Look Ahead

This early time, from 1800 to 1850, was just the beginning of the Chinese Australian story.

The search for gold

This first phase of Chinese migration was just the beginning.

In 1851, gold was discovered in Australia. This changed everything. Thousands of Chinese men came to search for gold and seek fortune. That is the story in the next book.

Before the gold rush, Chinese migrants were small in number but large in impact. They came during difficult times, worked hard and helped build the foundations of the Australian nation.

13. Remembering the Past

Today, we remember the bravery of those early Chinese migrants. They came to Australia in the early years of the colony. Travel was difficult, and the future was uncertain. They brought their culture, knowledge and strong family values.

Early Chinese Migrants

The gold rush

When gold was discovered in Australia in 1851, thousands more Chinese people came to the country hoping to find fortune. The gold rush changed everything.

Today, we remember the bravery of those first Chinese migrants. They came during hard times. They left their homes, crossed the ocean and worked in a new land. They brought their culture, knowledge and strong family values.

Their story helps us understand how migration has shaped Australia. People from all over the world have come here, worked hard and helped build the country we live in today.

We can thank the early Chinese Australians for their strength, courage, and contribution to our shared history.

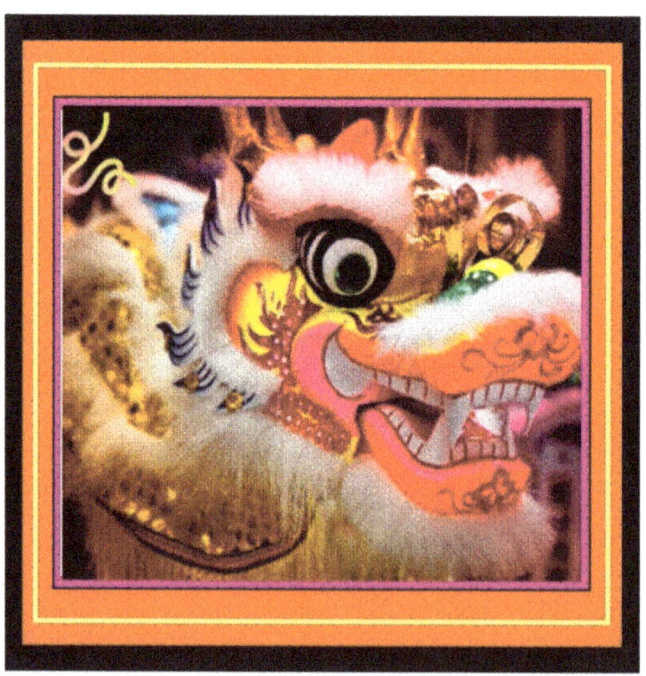

14. Timeline

1788	British occupation of Australia begins.
Early 1800s	Chinese sailors start arriving on trading ships.
1818	Mak Sai Ying (John Shying) arrives as first known Chinese settler.
1840	Convict transportation to NSW ends.
1848	First group of 120 Chinese workers arrives from Xiamen.
1850	Thousands more Chinese arrive before the gold rush.

GLOSSARY

Artisans — A worker in a skilled trade, especially someone that creates things by hand.

Indentured — Someone who is required to work by contract for another and for a certain period of time.

Migration — People moving from one country to settle in another.

Racism — Prejudice, discrimination, or antagonism by an individual, community, or institution against a person or people on the basis of their membership of a particular racial or ethnic group.

SOURCES

Grassby, Al & Hill, Marji (2000) *Chinese Australians*. South Yarra, Vic, Macmillan.

Hill, Marji 2022 *Gold and the Chinese: Racism, Riots and Protest on the Australian Goldfields.* Broadbeach, Qld, The Prison Tree Press. (Gold! Hidden Stories of Australia's Past, Book 3)

Mo Yimei (1988) "Harvest of Endurance: a History of the Chinese in Australia 1788-1988" Sydney, Australia-China Friendship Society. http://www.multiculturalaustralia.edu.au/doc/yimei_1.pdf

National Museum of Australia. "Early Chinese Migrants". https://www.nma.gov.au/explore/features/harvest-of-endurance/scroll/early-chinese-migrants

ABOUT MARJI HILL

Marji Hill runs her art career alongside her career as an author. She is a highly respected international author as well as a seasoned business executive, researcher and coach.

Marji is passionate about promoting understanding between Australia's First Nations people and other Australians. The spirit of reconciliation was fostered in all her writings ever since she was a Research Fellow in Education at the Australian Institute of Aboriginal and Torres Strait Islander Studies (AIATSIS) in Canberra.

From 2008 to 2011, Marji was Deputy Chairperson of the Mosman Branch of Reconciliation Australia in Sydney. Following her Research Fellowship at AIATSIS in 1976 Marji, together with her late partner, Alex Barlow, produced more than seventy (70) books on all aspects of the First Nations people including the critical, annotated bibliography *Black Australia*.

In 1989 she was the Project Coordinator and one of the researchers and writers of *Australian Aboriginal Culture* the official Australian Government publication on First Nations people.

In 1988 *Six Australian Battlefields* was published by Angus and Robertson. A decade later it was re-published by Allen & Unwin as a paperback edition. Her nine-volume encyclopaedia, *Macmillan*

Encyclopaedia of Australia's Aboriginal Peoples was published in 2000 and in 2009 she published *The Apology: Saying Sorry To The Stolen Generations*.

Marji's more recent publications extend to self-improvement and self-help with books like *Staying Young Growing Old* and *Inspired by Country* a self-help book about painting with gouache.

MORE BOOKS BY MARJI HILL

First Nations

Hill, Marji 2021 *Australian Aboriginal History: 5 Stories of Indigenous Heroes.* Broadbeach, Qld, The Prison Tree Press.

Hill, Marji 2021 *First People Then and Now: Introducing Indigenous Australians.* 2nd ed. Broadbeach, Qld, The Prison Tree Press.

Aboriginal Global Pioneers

Hill, Marji 2024 *Australian Aboriginal Origins: Earliest Beginnings.* Broadbeach, Qld, The Prison Tree Press. (Book 1)

Hill, Marji 2024 *Australian Aboriginal Trade: Sharing Goods and Services.* Broadbeach, Qld, The Prison Tree Press. (Book 2)

Hill, Marji 2024 *Australian Aboriginal Religion: Country and Dreaming.* Broadbeach, Qld, The Prison Tree Press. (Book 3)

Hill, Marji 2024 *Australian Aboriginal Fire: Managing Country.* Broadbeach, Qld, The Prison Tree Press. (Book 4)

Hill, Marji 2024 *Australian Aboriginal Medicine: Caring for People.* Broadbeach, Qld, The Prison Tree Press. (Book 5)

Self-improvement/Self-Help

Hill, Marji 2014 *Staying Young Growing Old.* Broadbeach, Qld, The Prison Tree Press.

Hill, Marji 2020 *How Big Is Your Why? An Author's Guide to Time Management and Productivity to Achieve Transformational Results.* Broadbeach, Qld, The Prison Tree Press.

Hill, Marji 2020 *A Create and Publish Toolbox: 101 Prompts In A Guided Journal To Help You Write, Self-publish, And Market Your Book on Amazon.* Broadbeach, Qld, The Prison Tree Press.

Hill, Marji 2021 *Inspired by Country: An Artist's Journey Back to Nature, Landscape Painting with Gouache.* Broadbeach, Qld, The Prison Tree Press.

Hill, Marji 2024 *Australian Paintings: Artworks by Marji Hill.* Broadbeach, Qld, The Prison Tree Press.

Gold

Hill, Marji 2022 *Gates of Gold: The Discovery of Gold, its Legacy and its Contribution to Australian Identity.* Broadbeach, Qld, The Prison Tree Press.

Hill, Marji 2022 *Shadows of Gold: Eureka and the Birth of Australian Democracy.* Broadbeach, Qld, The Prison Tree Press.

Hill, Marji 2022 *Gold and the Chinese: Racism, Riots and Protest on the Australian Goldfields.* Broadbeach, Qld, The Prison Tree Press.

Hill, Marji 2022 *Ghosts of Gold: The Life and Times of Jupiter Mosman.* Broadbeach, Qld, The Prison Tree Press.

Hill, Marji 2022 *Blood Gold: Native Police, Bushrangers & Law and Order on the Goldfields.* Broadbeach, Qld, The Prison Tree Press.

www.ingramcontent.com/pod-product-compliance
Lightning Source LLC
Chambersburg PA
CBHW061744290426
43661CB00129B/1086